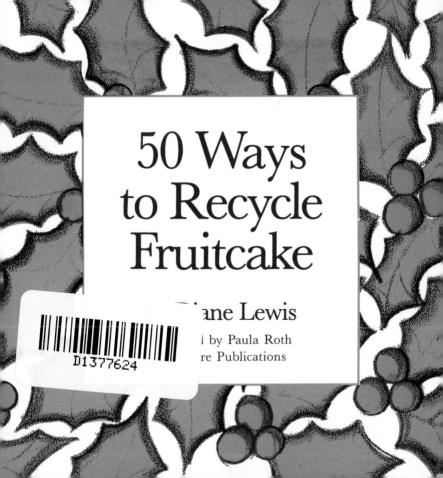

50 Ways to Recycle Fruitcake

Diane Lewis

by Paula Roth

Publications

This book is dedicated to
Craig, Matthew, Chad and Ryan
for always adding spice to my life.

Copyright © 1992 by Diane Rathnow Lewis

Published by
Adventure Publications, Inc.
P.O. Box 296
Cambridge, MN 55008

ISBN 0-934860-94-7

A Few Words About Fruitcake.

Fruitcake has been part of civilization since before recorded history. If you are fortunate enough to travel to China — check out that Great Wall! And do you know that anthropologists found buried in the tombs of the great Pharaohs of Egypt? Yes, fruitcake. Theory has it that the secret of the Great Fruitcake was used as part of the mummification process. The ancient roads of Rome and Athens are made of stone? I think not! And those quaint cobblestone streets of merry old England — you're right. Fruitcake. It is not only possible for us to carry on this ancient practice of recycling fruitcake, indeed it's a necessity. While loss of the ozone layer and destruction of the rainforests are serious threats, the thought of being overcome by fruitcakes is also frightful. We must do all we can to prevent such a fate and to this end, we offer fifty practical tips on how to recycle that fruitcake.

Help the
Highway
Department!
Fruitcake makes
an indestructible
pothole filler.

Local airports can use fruitcake to chock planes at the terminal.

At home, use your fruitcakes for doorstops, footscrapers, bookends and lamp bases.

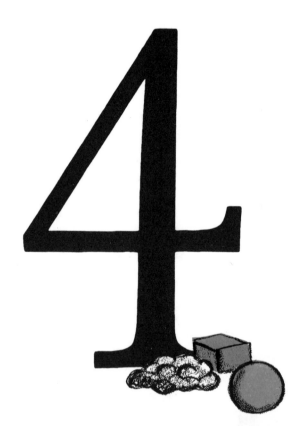

Slices of fruitcake make excellent coasters.

For the health and fitness addict – save time and money at the gym. Use your fruitcake as part of your weight resistance program

The horticulturalist can design and build a fruitcake garden in the same fashion as a rock garden. Fruitcake also makes an attractive edging for a flower bed.

We must do our part to conserve water. A fruitcake placed in your toilet tank will save thousands of gallons of water each year.

And remember when it's time for anchors-aweigh; have a machine shop drill a hole in your fruitcake, attach a strong rope and voila! Great anchor!

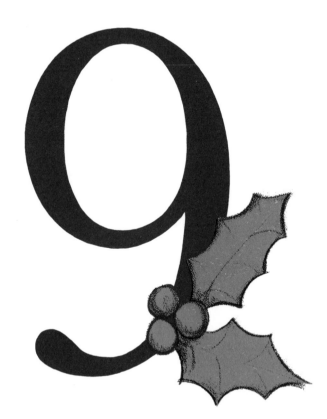

Fruitcake also makes wonderful ballast for your boat.

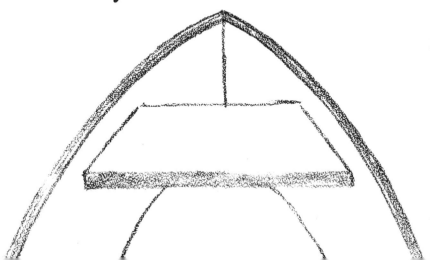

Donate your fruitcake to an urban restoration program. It's an invaluable building material and is good for foundation work.

If you dread driving in the snow, a few fruitcakes in your trunk will give you excellent traction.

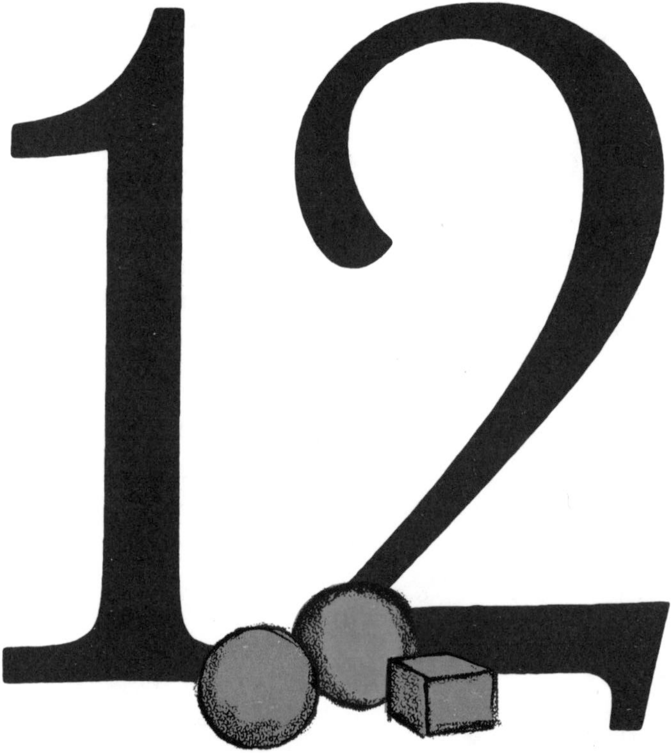
12

Your fruitcakes can be used to build highway sound barriers or lovely privacy fences.

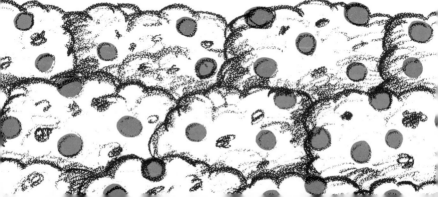

If you have a leaky basement, you may be interested to know that fruitcake has excellent waterproofing qualities.

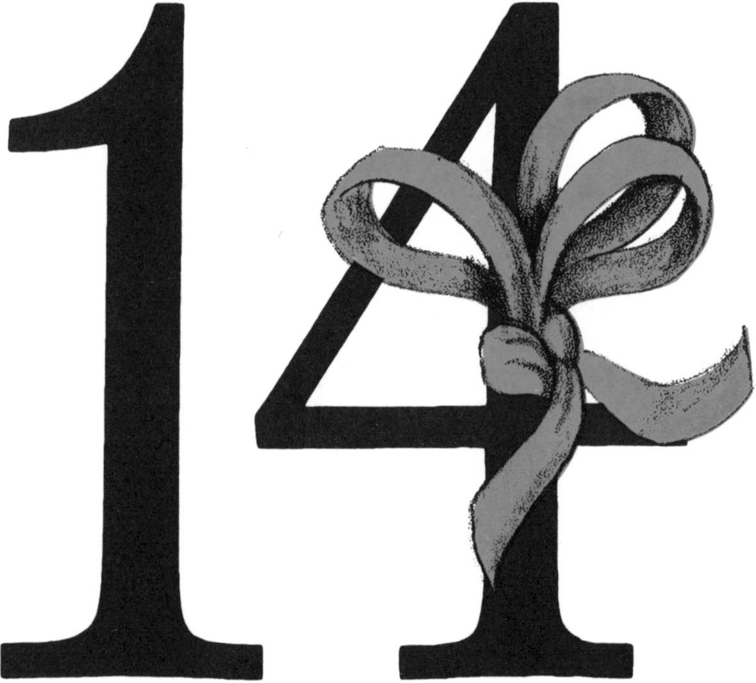
14

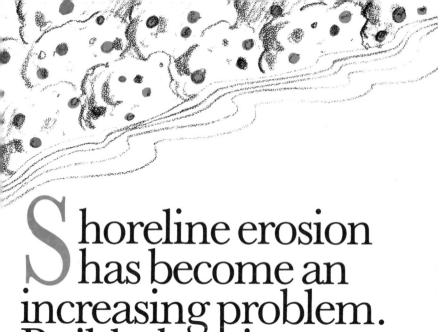

Shoreline erosion has become an increasing problem. Build a hurricane-proof sea wall with your fruitcake.

15

Two-inch slices of fruitcake make space-age attic insulation. It has an "R" rating of 641.

16

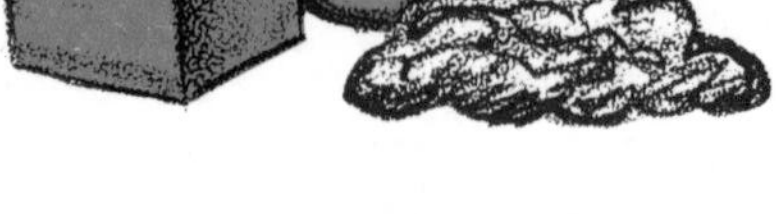

For the outdoor gourmet...Use fruitcake to replace those tired lava rocks in your barbecue pit next summer.

17

D o you have a wobbly table leg? Thin slices of fruitcake placed under the leg will eliminate that wobble forever.

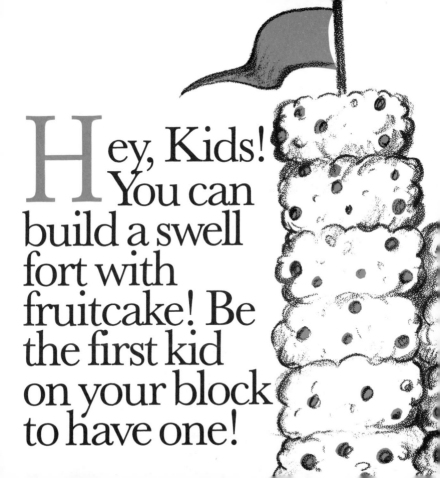

Hey, Kids! You can build a swell fort with fruitcake! Be the first kid on your block to have one!

One more
landscape design
idea; build a beautiful
patio using fruitcake. It
will not crack
or heave
in winter.

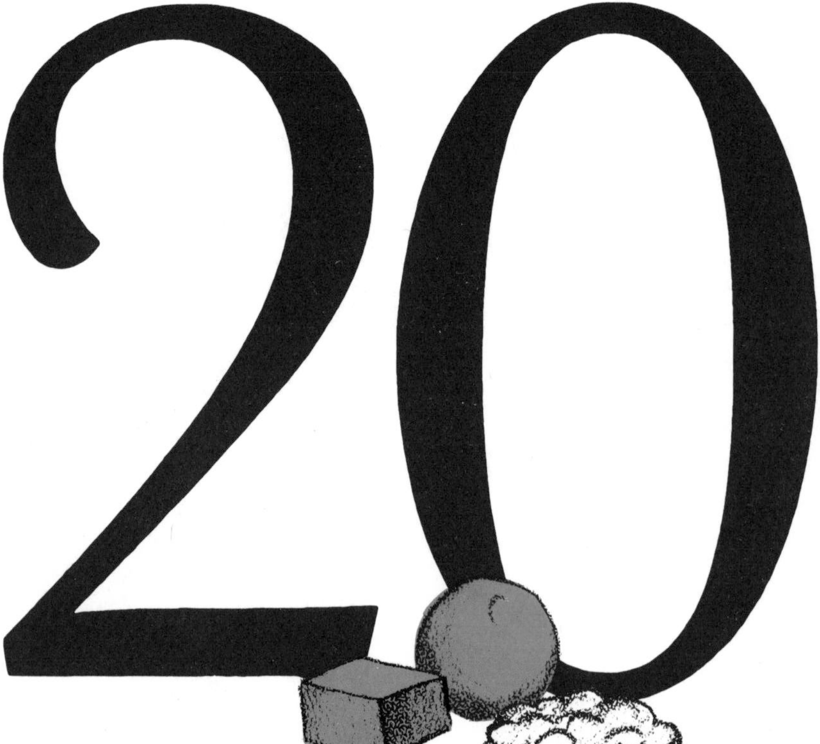
20

A 1" x 1" square of fruitcake makes an excellent double-sided adhesive for mounting wall hangings. It won't harm walls. Great for apartments.

Stop those throw rugs from sliding. Simply rub a little fruitcake on the back side and the rugs will stay in place.

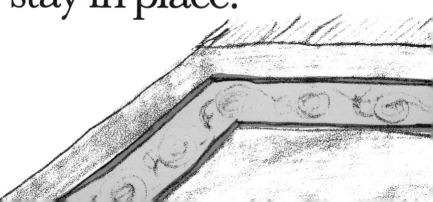

You'll really get a bang out of this one! Try slices of fruitcake the next time you go skeet shooting. You'll never use a clay pigeon again!

23

Though it has
not yet received
NHL sanction,
sliced fruitcake
makes excellent
hockey pucks.

24

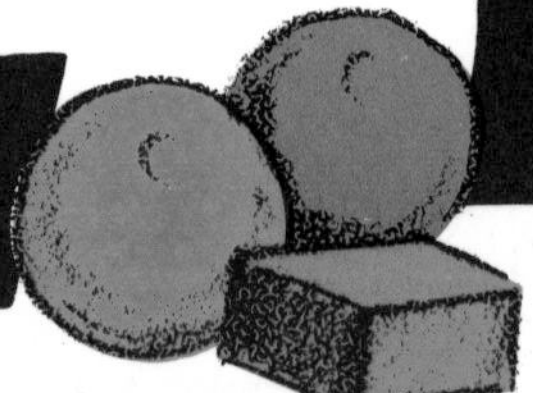

Is your car ready for a new set of brakes? Advise your mechanic that you want fruitcake used for your brake pads. They will out-last your car.

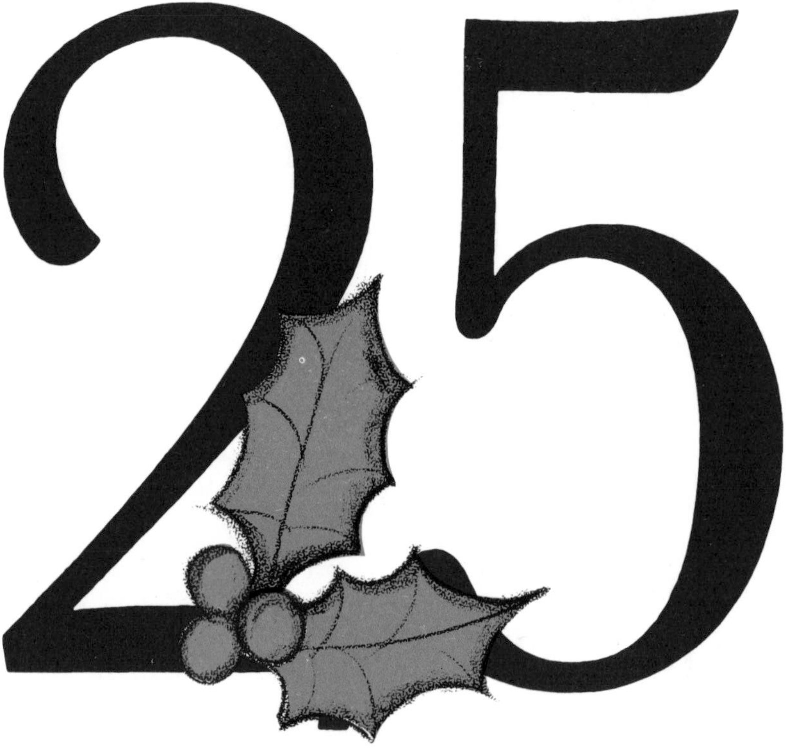
25

Nothing removes dry skin from heels and elbows better than a hunk of fruitcake. Gentle to the skin but effective on those calluses.

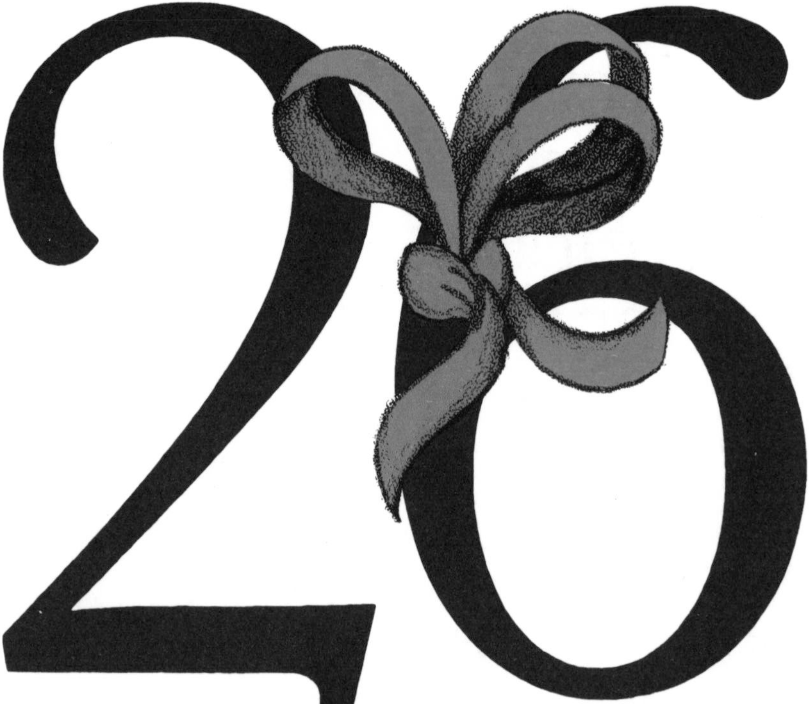

Very thin pieces of fruitcake make environmentally-safe fly strips.

Thin stamp-size pieces of fruitcake make an interesting alternative to sealing wax on your correspondence.

28

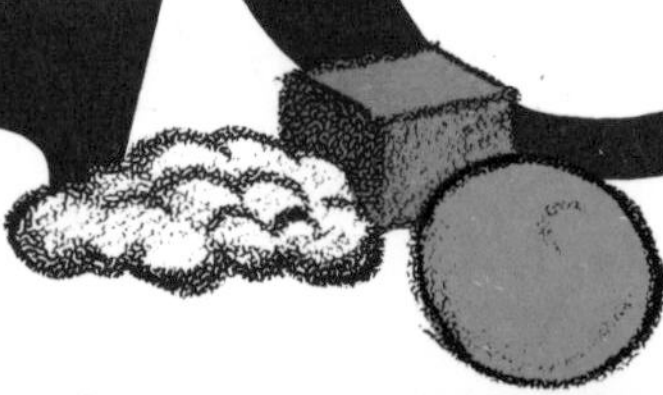

Did the cork from your good bottle of wine break? Use a plug of fruitcake! Reopen it with your corkscrew; the fruitcake won't crack or crumble.

Have your lapidary shop cut and polish your heirloom fruitcake and set the pieces in fine gold mountings for very unusual rings, pendants and earrings.

Protect your valuables with fruitcake. A wall safe made with fruitcake bricks is fireproof, waterproof and burglarproof.

Next time you need to tenderize a tough piece of meat, your fruitcake can be the best tool in your kitchen!

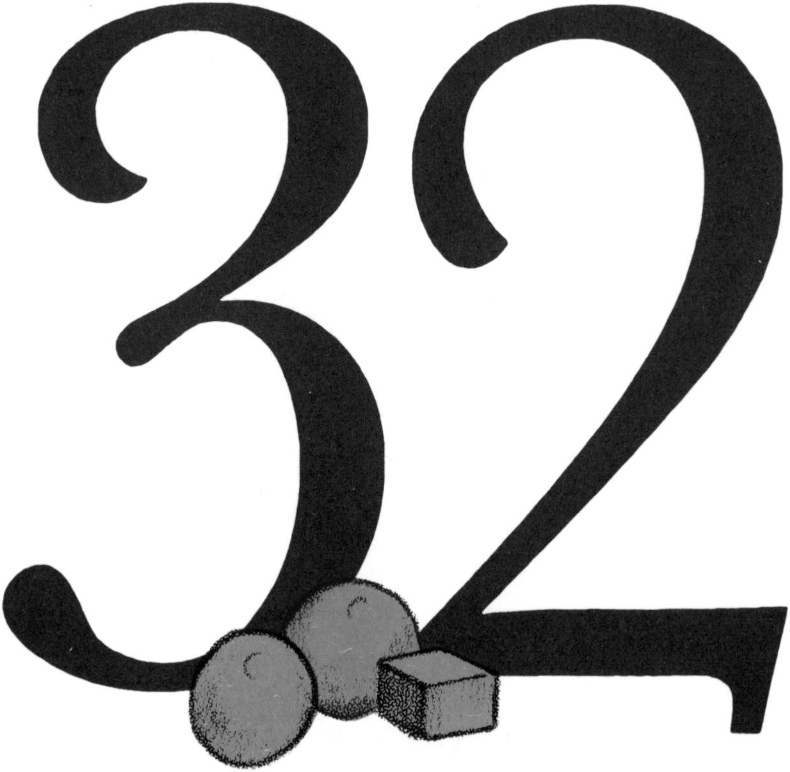
32

For boxers and football players, fruitcake makes excellent mouth guards.

For devotees of the martial arts, try the challenge of breaking a fruitcake with your karate chop. Requires much more concentration than wood or even cinder blocks.

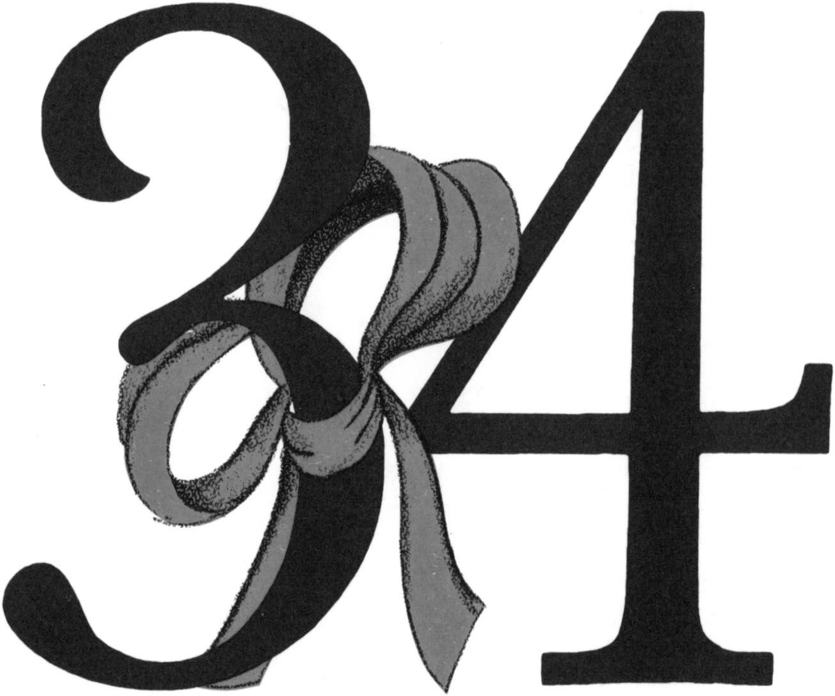
34

On cold winter nights, heat a fruitcake in your oven and tuck it under the covers as a foot warmer. It will retain heat for up to 9 hours.

35

Now that we all are recycling, use your fruitcake to flatten aluminum cans. Works better than the expensive mechanical kind and helps to relieve stress, too!

36

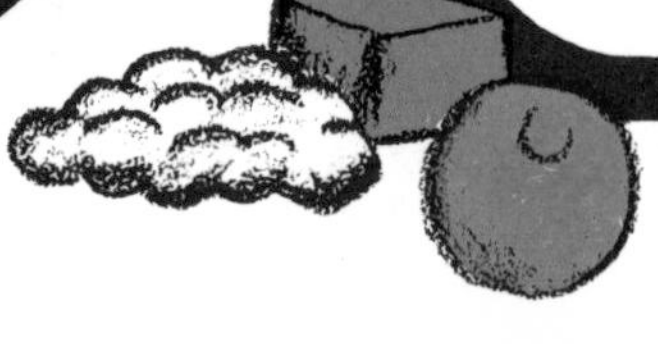

A hollowed-out fruitcake makes an excellent time capsule destined to preserve artifacts for centuries.

37

Ichthyologists agree that fruitcake that has been drilled and/or carved makes excellent aquarium decorations.

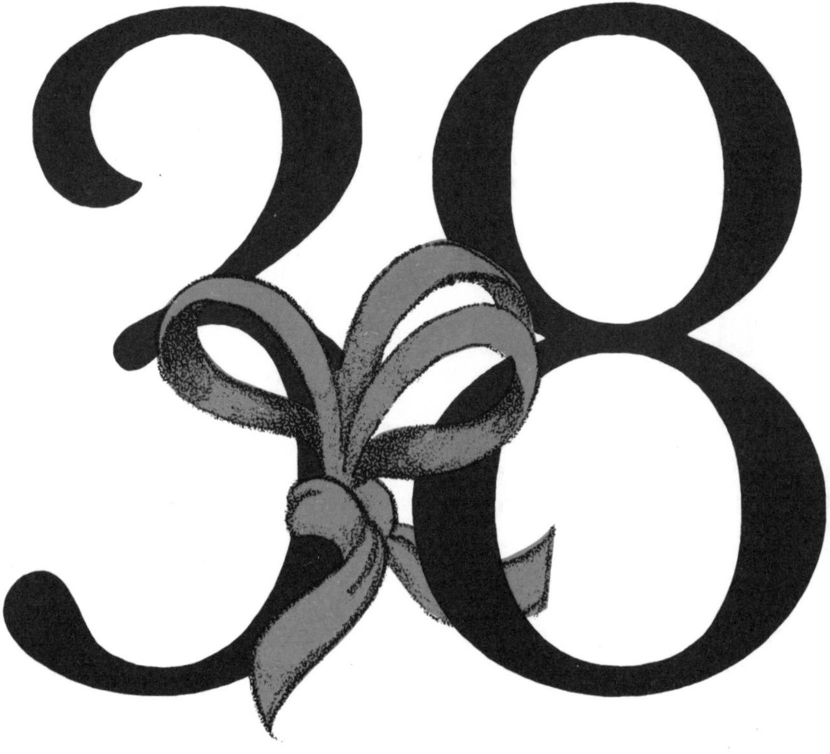
38

A fruitcake sliced in half and hinged makes a festive and effective nutcracker.

Oil spill on your garage floor? Slices of fruitcake will soak up that mess in no time!

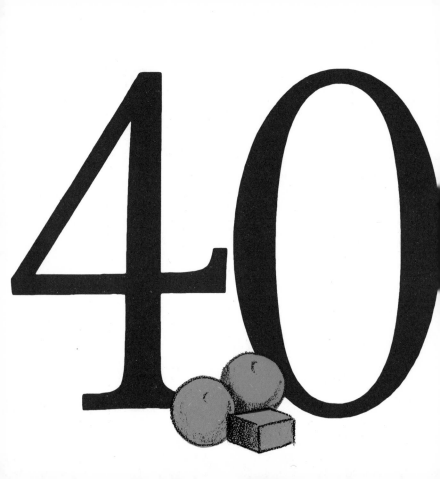

Consider parquet flooring! Sliced fruitcake flooring is not only self-adhesive, but also resists scuff marks, never needs polishing and adds stylish color & texture.

Having problems in your yard with moles or gophers? Simply drop fruitcake into the entry holes of these little rodents' burrows. You'll never see them again. And fruitcake is more humane than traps.

Saving the memories of summer by pressing flowers has just become easier. No need to fuss with thick books . . . your fruitcake makes an excellent flower press.

Fruitcake slices make exceptional mounting boards for bug and butterfly specimens. No need to pin those delicate wings.

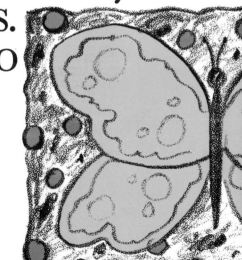

We can save California! Donate your fruitcake to geologists to fill in the San Andreas Fault, save our west coast from seismographic destruction.

NASA is planning to use fruitcake in the space program! Since it is the only thing that will not float in space, it will anchor objects in spacecraft cabins.

Want to scare little kids at Halloween? Hand out slices of fruitcake when they come to your door. Trick or Treat.

Effectively stop runs in panty-hose by smearing a bit of fruitcake on your hosiery. Works better than clear nail polish.

You will never find a better lint remover than a slice of good ol' fruitcake. Removes pet hair, lint and dandruff in a snap.

Replace one or two of those common every-day glass windows in your home with a window made from slices of fruitcake for that beautiful stained-glass effect.

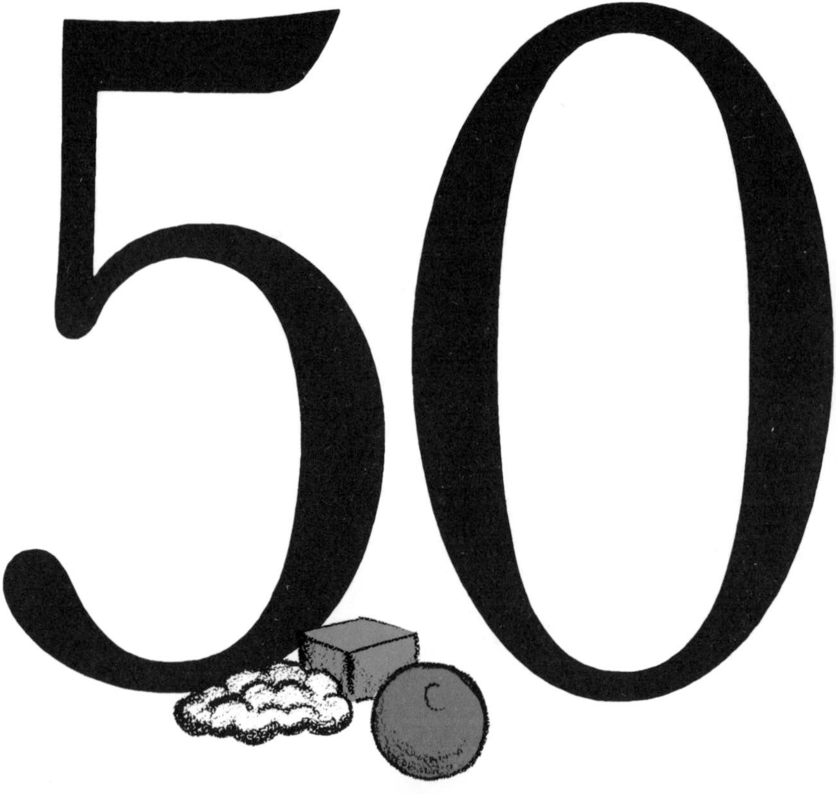
50

As a last resort, you may try to eat your fruitcake. We have sworn testimony from six living people attesting to the palatable qualities of fruitcake. (They may have been forged.)

For More Information...

The *Fruitcake Recycling Council* is dedicated to providing reliable information on safe fruitcake recycling and to developing a nation-wide network for fruitcake recyclers. We offer assistance to local groups and municipalities concerned with the long-term ramifications of fruitcake. The *Fruitcake Recycling Council* is constantly conducting research with a goal of finding new ways to deal with fruitcake. Despite our extensive research, there are still many unanswered questions regarding fruitcake. Part of our mission is to dispel the rumor that there is only one fruitcake and it is simply passed around from year to year. This kind of thinking only complicates the problem. In fact, right here in America there is a quiet town of two thousand people that claims the title of *Fruitcake Capital of the World*. Claxton, Georgia reportedly produced more commercially-made fruitcake than any other place on the face of the earth. The question that immediately comes to mind is: On what platform did the mayor of this small metropolis run? Was it built from fruitcake? And could they, in good conscience, celebrate a fruitcake festival?

And then there is the ethical issue of baking something that has a potential life-span longer than your own. In *Joy of Cooking*, authors Irma S. Rombauer and Marion Rombauer Becker tell us of fruitcake that can be soaked in liquor, buried in powdered sugar and enjoyed as long as 25 years after baking. Please explain the logic of this.

We invite your comments or stories about how you have dealt with fruitcake. Your story could help millions of others who are trying to cope with this annual problem. We would like to thank you in advance for your help in our cause.

And so the *Fruitcake Recycling Council* stands firm in its conviction to conquer the control of fruitcake. For more information on how to start a fruitcake recycling center in your area, please write:

Fruitcake Recycling Council
c/o Adventure Publications
P.O. Box 269
Cambridge, MN 55008
Be sure to enclose a stamped, self-addressed envelope.

About the Author

Diane Lewis spent her formative years obediently unloading the semi-trailers of candied cherries, citron, pineapple and raisins that came to her home each fall for the traditional Great Fruitcake Ritual. But one day she saw a vision in a huge tub of fruitcake batter. From this mystical experience, she knew how she could make the world a better place, how she could make a difference. As founder of the FRUITCAKE RECYCLING COUNCIL, she actively works to educate the public in ways to control and hopefully one day eliminate fruitcake from our planet.

In her spare time, Diane became a successful writer/inventor/entrepreneur with such products to her credit as The Recycled Fruitcake Ornament™, Capsule Critters™, Money to Burn™ and Treasury Notes™ to name a few.

She resides in Livonia, Michigan with her husband and three sons.